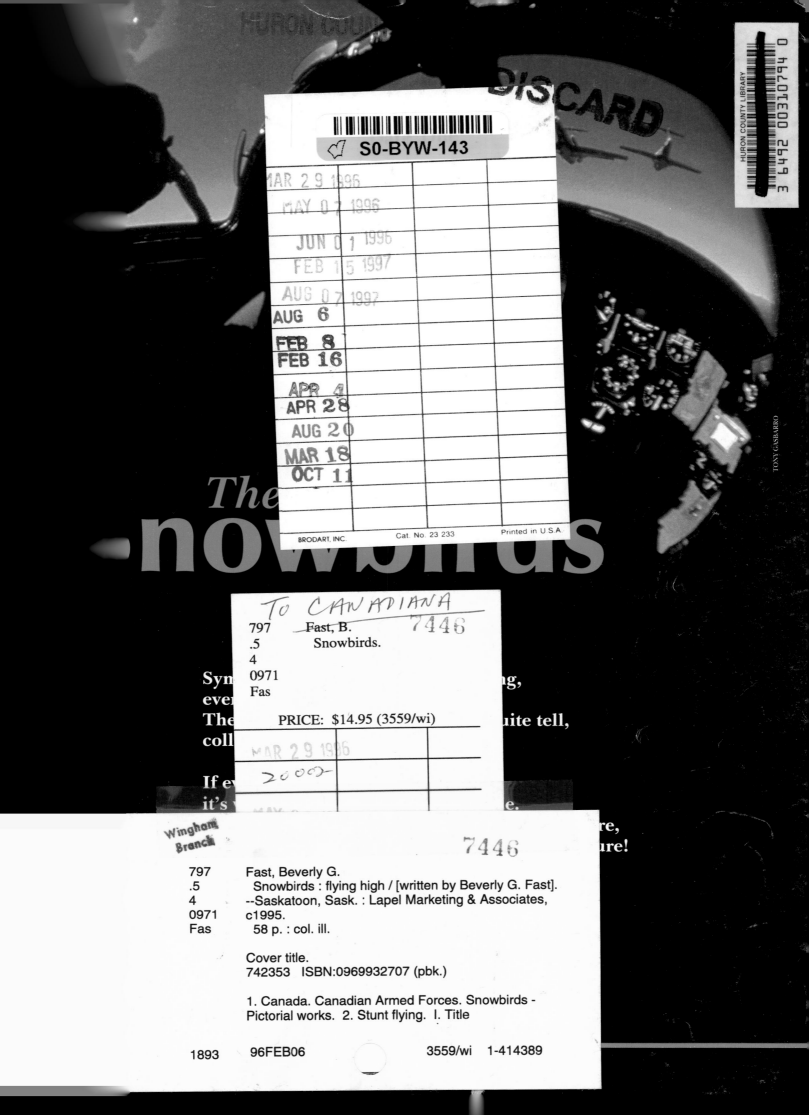

HURON COUNTY

DISCARD

TONY GASBARRO

The

nowbirds

Syn... ...ng,
ever...
The... ...uite tell,
coll...

If ev...
it's v... ...e.

...re,
...ure!

Prime Minister
of Canada

It is with great pleasure that I extend my warmest greetings to everyone associated with the publication of this tribute to the Snowbirds, in honour of their 25th anniversary. I know that its readers will find the history of the team both admirable and compelling.

For twenty-five years, the Snowbirds have amazed and delighted audiences with the prowess and artistry of their aerial manoeuvres. The white-streaked skies above Parliament Hill on Canada Day are an unforgettable sight for anyone with the good fortune to witness the exploits of this dedicated team of flyers.

I would like to take this opportunity to offer my congratulations to the Commanding Officer and the members of the Snowbirds on this special anniversary. Please accept my best wishes for every success, now and in the future.

Jean Chrétien

Jean Chrétien
Prime Minister
OTTAWA
1995

Premier of Saskatchewan

I take great pleasure in introducing this special publication in recognition of the 25th Anniversary of the Canadian Forces 431 Air Demonstration Squadron, the Snowbirds.

This publication commemorates 25 years of outstanding performances by the Snowbirds and I commend the team's past and present members for their exceptional skill, hard work and commitment. The pilots exhibit true courage and unerring judgment and are central to the drama of the Snowbirds. Their difficult and precise manoeuvres have thrilled fans throughout the world, and the people of our province are proud that these renowned aviators are such excellent ambassadors for Saskatchewan.

It is certainly exciting to see the Snowbirds suddenly appear in formation from out of the prairie sky. Nature has blessed our province with seemingly endless blue skies that are the perfect setting for the team's electrifying aerodynamic displays. The Saskatchewan landscape demands the qualities of cooperation and dedication from our people, and these qualities are captured in the Snowbirds' fine-tuned precision flying.

The accuracy and daring of this highly skilled team are recognized with deep admiration wherever it performs and I take enormous pride in introducing this beautiful Anniversary book. Saskatchewan is honoured to have been home to the team for the last 25 years, and we look forward to being their home for many more years to come.

Roy Romanow.

Roy Romanow
Premier

Saskatchewan *90th*
1905 - 1995

FEB 21 '96

Canadian Forces Air Command

Within the Air Force, a "25th Anniversary" is of special significance. It is at this point in history that a quarter-century of dedicated service is recognized. Although 431 Air Demonstration Squadron has yet to reach this milestone, this year does mark the 25th year that the white Tutor aircraft of the Snowbirds have performed in the skies overhead. While there have been numerous aerobatic and flight demonstration teams throughout the history of the Air Force, none have had the longevity and record of service of the Snowbirds.

Over the years the Snowbirds have enjoyed outstanding success while establishing themselves as one of the world's foremost jet formation aerobatic teams. In addition to their skill in the air, the Snowbirds also excel as goodwill ambassadors for Canada and the Canadian Forces. However, their contribution to the Air Force and Canada goes far beyond mere showmanship. Their involvement with the Canadian Injury Prevention Foundation through its "Heroes" program and "Stupid Line Campaign" promotes smart risk for young people. The Snowbirds serve as role models for the five key messages: get trained, wear the gear, buckle up, drive sober and look first.

The dedication, spirit and efficiency of both the air and ground crew serve as an example for today's Air Force. The men and women of this unique unit can take great pride in their achievements over the past quarter-century for their efforts have brought enjoyment to millions of people world wide. A true Canadian symbol, I look forward to their next 25 years.

G. Scott Clements
Lieutenant-General
Commander

15 Wing
Moose Jaw

It is with great pleasure and pride as a Canadian that I congratulate
431 Air Demonstration Squadron, the Snowbirds, on their 25th Anniversary.
Canada's Air Force has a proud heritage of some 66 years of aerobatic display
teams, starting with the Siskins in 1929 and leading to today's Snowbirds. After
a quarter of a century of thrilling millions of airshow spectators across Canada
and the United States, the Snowbirds have become a de facto national symbol
and are magnificent goodwill ambassadors for all Canadians. Their reputation
for excellence extends around the globe.

During three years at Moose Jaw, I have watched three successive groups of
airmen at 431 Squadron evolve into Snowbirds teams. The moulding of each
group of pilots, aircraft technicians and support personnel, beginning each
November, into a new team that is ready to start the airshow circuit in May
demonstrates graphically the power of team spirit and represents the epitome
of teamwork.

We have all seen the Snowbirds in action in the air, but few have had the
opportunity to get a behind-the-scenes look at the people, the intensity and
the amount of work that it takes to present a world-calibre aerobatic display
with nine jet aircraft. This books tells that story but, more importantly, it is
about the people, their families and the supporting cast that make it all
happen.

Congratulations to all members of the Snowbirds, past and present, on your
25 years of excellence.

W.A. Kalbfleisch

W.A. Kalbfleisch
Colonel
Commander

Canadian Forces
431 AD Squadron

It is indeed a privilege and an honour to lead the Snowbirds through this, the 25th Anniversary season, and to have the opportunity to contribute to the proud heritage which began with the RCAF Siskins in 1929. The 1995 Snowbirds represent the culmination of 25 years of tradition, teamwork, and excellence.

By the end of the 25th Air Display season, the Snowbirds will have performed approximately 1400 airshows in front of more than 80 million people. These Air Displays have taken the team from the Arctic Circle to Southern Mexico, and from coast to coast in both Canada and the United States.

The Snowbirds truly epitomize the teamwork and dedication that exists in the Canadian Forces. The Squadron is, in fact, a reflection of Canadian culture, as the teams' members come from all regions of the country. The Snowbirds are an excellent example of what is possible when Canadians work together toward a common goal.

I am sure Canadians are proud of the Snowbirds' reputation as one of the world's finest military jet formation aerobatic teams, and as outstanding ambassadors for Canada.

S.P. Hill
Major
Commanding Officer

RUSS HEINL.

25 Years of Aerobatic Excellence
Canada's Snowbirds

Contents

Skill, dedication, excellence. For 25 years, Canada's Snowbirds have thrilled audiences with their displays of precision aerobatics.

As millions of airshow spectators prove every year, the thrill of watching Snowbirds' aircraft soaring and diving in the sky never fades. Bomb bursts, head-on solo passes, cross-overs, rolls – their unique brand of flying has won the Canadian Forces 431 AD Squadron, the Snowbirds, fans around the world.

The team represents a quarter century of air demonstration excellence, a legacy unequalled in Canada. This book is a tribute to Snowbirds past and present; to their skill in the air, their dedicated goodwill efforts on the ground, and their excellence as a symbol of Canadian unity and pride.

twenty-five years

Inset: Canada's first military aerobatic team, the Siskins, flew single engine biplanes.

Main: The RCAF Golden Hawks (1959-63) soared across the sky in powerful F-86 Sabres.

Siskins to Centennaires

A Proud History of Aerobatics

The RCAF Golden Centennaires were formed in 1967 to celebrate Canada's Centennial. They began with nine Tutor aircraft, but when an accident early in the year claimed the life of one pilot, the team flew only eight Tutors.

Since the day in 1929 when three Royal Canadian Air Force biplanes put on the first public display of precision air force flying, Canadian aviation has never been the same. The aircraft were front line fighter planes, the pride of the RCAF: Armstrong Whitworth Siskin IIIA biplanes. Powered by a single 450 horse power engine, the Siskins had a ceiling of 27,000 feet and a top speed of 156 miles per hour. Together, the three planes and their pilots made up the Trans Canada Air Pageant Team – the Siskins – Canada's first national air demonstration team.

The Siskins were born at RCAF Station Camp Borden in Ontario. For three years, they delighted audiences across Canada with their feats of aerial derring-do. One manoeuvre called for a low level pass with all three planes flying abreast and tied together by a single length of rope. It was this kind of heart-stopping flying that earned the Siskins an international reputation for skill and showmanship. When the team disbanded in 1931, no one dreamed it would be 27 long years before Canada had another national aerobatics team.

Military air demonstration teams did not experience a rebirth until after World War II. In 1949, the RCAF Blue Devils, based in St. Hubert, Quebec, took to the skies in silver and blue de Havilland Vampire jets, the first jet aircraft in RCAF squadron service. This regional team remained together for two seasons, performing in major airshows in Toronto, Ottawa and Chicago.

twenty-five years

Other regional teams followed: in 1950, the RCAF Easy Aces, flying Harvard aircraft, performed across southwestern Ontario; in 1954, the RCAF Prairie Pacific Team flew F-86s and T-33s in shows across western Canada.

In Europe, air demonstration teams were established to display Canada's participation in NATO. The RCAF Fireballs in 1954 and the Sky Lancers in 1955 both flew Canadian Mark V Sabres, better known as the F-86. Most regional teams were disbanded after one year, but the Sky Lancers managed to regroup in 1956. A disastrous crash during a training exercise later that year killed all four pilots, sending shock waves through the military and bringing all aerobatic displays to a sudden halt.

RCAF pilots continued to fly, and to test the very limits of their aircraft and themselves – that was their job. They did not give up hope, however, that the ban on aerobatic teams would be lifted. Military decision-makers also recognized that such teams provided pilots with an excellent opportunity to hone their skills to the highest level. So in 1959, three years after the Sky Lancers' accident, the RCAF returned to aerobatics.

First, the RCAF Red Knight charged across the sky, performing solo aerobatics in a T-33 jet painted fire-engine red. Then came the RCAF Golden Hawks, the military's first national aerobatics team since the Siskins.

The Golden Hawks were created to help celebrate the Golden Anniversary of Flight in Canada, and the 35th Anniversary of the Royal Canadian Air Force, or RCAF. From their home base in Chatham, New Brunswick, the 6-plane team travelled to airshows across Canada and the United States.

The Big Diamond formation, the Snowbirds signature, was performed over 25 years ago by the RCAF Golden Centennaires.

After 27 years without a national team, the Golden Hawks seemed determined to make up for lost time. In their sleek gold and red F-86 Sabre jets, they dazzled spectators with displays of precision flying and some of the tightest formations ever flown.

Of course compared to the Siskin, the F-86 was a rocket. Designed and built by Canadair in Montreal, it could produce more than 7,000 lbs of thrust and achieve speeds of more than 700 mph. The Golden Hawks' highly trained, highly skilled pilots were able to harness this raw power. Their performances consisted of a series of loops, rolls, cross-overs and bomb bursts – all standard RCAF manoeuvres. Yet when the Golden Hawks performed them, they were executed in close formation.

Tight formation flying became the team's hallmark, winning them national and international acclaim. The first year proved such a success that the team was expanded to seven planes. This allowed for more versatile and eye-catching performances with five-plane formations and two opposing solos.

Despite their popularity, the Golden Hawks were disbanded in 1963 after 317 performances. Nonetheless, the team had earned a place for Canada on the world aerobatics stage, right alongside the Blue Angels of the U.S. Navy and the Red Arrows of the British RAF.

ED DRADER

While the Golden Hawks were in their heyday, a new regional team popped into existence – the RCAF Goldilocks. The team was made up of RCAF instructors from CFB Moose Jaw. In their bright yellow Harvard trainers, the Goldilocks flew comic performances billed as interpretations of their students' attempts at formation flying. Audiences loved them, but the Air Force was not amused. In 1963, their second year, the Goldilocks were told to drop their name and curtail their performances. The team disbanded in 1964.

For airshow fans across Canada, the next three years were frustrating. There were still exciting performances to see, but the teams were American or European. Canadians had grown accustomed to seeing their nation represented at these shows, and represented well. Many wanted to feel that pride again.

In 1967, Canada marked its centennial anniversary with a variety of special events and projects, including the creation of a new air demonstration team based in Portage la Prairie, Manitoba. They were called the RCAF Golden Centennaires, and they were brought together for one year only in honour of the Centennial, and the 50th year of Military Aviation in Canada. By year's end, the Centennaires had accomplished much more than expected. In addition to 100 Centennial performances, they had flown the opening and closing ceremonies of Expo '67 in Montreal, performed at four show sites in the United States, and introduced over 4 million North American spectators to an exciting new style of formation flying.

What made the Centennaires unique was their choice of aircraft: CL-41 Tutor jets, painted blue and gold. In going with the small Tutor over the

The Snowbirds pay tribute to the whimsical aerobatic antics of the RCAF Goldilocks (1962-64) with the Goldilocks formation.

more powerful F-86, the Centennaires chose agility over muscle. This meant several things. First, the team flew larger formations – nine aircraft instead of the usual four or five. Second, they performed a wider variety of manoeuvres in much closer formation. Third, they were able to stay in front of the audience, at show centre so to speak, for more of the performance.

To add to the excitement, many Centennaires shows included demonstrations by the RCAF Red Knight soloist, a CF-104 Starfighter and CF-101 Voodoo solo duet, and two vintage World War II Avro 504Ks. It was a European-style show with a distinctly Canadian flavour, and it thrilled audiences from coast-to-coast.

Despite many letters of support and appreciation, the Centennaires were disbanded on schedule at the end of the 1967 airshow season. The Tutors were stripped of their Centennial colours and returned to duty as trainers at CFB Moose Jaw, where they were spotted by a sharp-eyed Base Commander. But that's another story ...

1969

Col O.B. Philip, former CO of Golden Centennaires is new Base Commander at CFB Moose Jaw.

1970

Unofficial formation flying demonstration team called 2CFFTS formed at CFB Moose Jaw.

1971

2CFFTS gets new name: *the Snowbirds.*

1972

Snowbirds increased to 9 Tutor aircraft. Full-time groundcrew assigned. Capt Lloyd Waterer killed during airshow in Trenton, Ontario.

1973

Snowbirds recognized as "official" team. Debut performance in United States a success.

1974

Team attains full aerobatic status, become first North American team to perform north of the Arctic Circle.

1975

Snowbirds made separate unit of the Canadian Forces at CFB Moose Jaw.

1976

Team performs at American Bicentennial celebration in Philadelphia, and at 1976 Summer Olympics in Montreal.

1977

Snowbirds become first Canadian air demonstration team to become permanent unit of Canadian Forces.

1978

Snowbirds achieve squadron status, a milestone in Canadian aviation history. Capt Gordon de Jong killed during airshow in Grande Prairie, Alberta.

1982

Snowbirds perform flypast at constitution repatriation ceremony on Parliament Hill.

1986

Snowbird #1 leads historic 5-plane international flypast at Abbotsford Airshow.

1987

Snowbirds win Art Scholl Memorial Showmanship Award given by the International Council of Airshows in Las Vegas, Nevada.

1988

Rare winter performance at Opening Ceremonies of Winter Olympics in Calgary, Alberta. Capt Wes Mackay killed in car accident.

1989

Capt Shane Antaya killed after mid-air collision sends his aircraft crashing into Lake Ontario at CNE show in Toronto.

1990

Snowbirds celebrate their 20th anniversary.

1991

Team makes cameo appearance with U.S. Navy Blue Angels at Disney World's 20th anniversary.

1992

Snowbirds serve as official Ambassadors of Canada 125 celebrations.

1993

Snowbirds are first Canadian Forces aerobatics team to perform in Mexico.

1995

Team members and fans around the world celebrate 25 years of Snowbirds air demonstration excellence.

BILL JOHNSON

RAFE TOMSETT

On a Wing and a Prayer

The Snowbirds 1971 - 1995

Canada has a long tradition of air demonstration excellence. Canadian Forces 431 Air Demonstration Squadron, the Snowbirds, are part of that proud heritage. They are the first Canadian Forces aerobatics team to achieve squadron status, the first to reach their 25th anniversary, and the first to perform north of the Arctic Circle and south of the Rio Grand. The story of their amazing success is one of survival against the odds.

twenty-five years

I t began in 1969 with the arrival of a new Base Commander at CFB Moose Jaw, Saskatchewan, home of the No. 2CFFTS, Canadian Forces Flying Training School, or The Big 2. The man was Colonel O.B. Philip, former Commanding Officer of the Golden Centennaires.

On his first tour of the base, Col Philip noticed five Tutor jets. The Tutors were not unusual in themselves – for almost 30 years, every Canadian Forces pilot has received their flight training on a Tutor – it was the white paint job. Trainers were normally an unpainted metallic silver. Col Philip was told the white Tutors were actually his old Centennaires, stripped of their colours, but still carrying the modifications necessary for aerobatics.

When Col Philip learned this, he quietly set to work re-establishing a Canadian Forces air demonstration team. He knew from his days as a Golden Centennaire that such a team could be a tremendous asset to the military and to Canada. He was not alone in this belief, but he was the only one with access to modified Tutors.

Col Philip did not have an official mandate to organize a team, so he formed an unofficial group called the 2CFFTS. It consisted of four aircraft and several volunteer instructors from the base.

In the summer of 1970, the team was invited to perform at the well-known Abbotsford Airshow in

> **Philip wryly described the fledgling team as "an unofficial formation demonstration team created to maintain instructor pilot efficiency."**

"It must be scary when you fly, because you are so close together. For one of the moves, the announcer said your wings are only 1 metre apart. Now that's close for jets to fly!" From a fan letter, one of hundreds received and answered by the team every year.

British Columbia. It was the public's first glimpse of what was to become the Snowbirds.

By the following spring, Col Philip had succeeded in getting the rest of the old Centennaire Tutors, which had been in storage in Ontario, transferred to CFB Moose Jaw. This brought the 2CFFTS up to seven planes.

In June of 1971, the 2CFFTS began their search for a more catchy name. It came from young Doug Farmer, a student at the base elementary school where a "Name the Team" contest had been held. Doug's entry was *the Snowbirds*.

The team flew under their new name for the first time on July 11 at the Saskatchewan Homecoming Airshow. The performance was distinguished not by stunts – the team was not cleared to perform aerobatics – but by formations flown in tight unison.

The addition of two solo aircraft in 1972 gave a new dimension to Snowbirds performances. Airshow audiences were familiar with four and five-plane formations, but nine planes was something new. The Snowbirds seemed to fill the sky.

With the increase in size, a full-time groundcrew was assigned for the show season and a competition held among base instructors. From now on, pilots had to win their place on the team through a demonstration of skill and training.

Flying is dangerous business, and early in the 1972 season the Snowbirds suffered their first fatality. The two solos were performing a low level cross-over at an airshow in Trenton, Ontario. The manoeuvre called for the aircraft to miss each other by about fifty feet, but one plane rolled too far and there was a mid-air collision. Capt Mike Marynowski was able to land safely, but Capt Lloyd Waterer, 24, died when his plane crashed into the ground.

It was a devastating loss. In a tribute to their teammate, the Snowbirds said, "he was a professional pilot in that he lived to fly and flew to live. His thirst to be airborne was only exceeded by the comradeship he offered to his fellowman."

The Snowbirds flew the rest of the season in an eight-plane formation. By the end of 1972, Canadians from coast-to-coast had been introduced to this dedicated team of gallant young men.

In 1973, the team won approval to include aerobatics in the show, although formation changes during manoeuvres were still prohibited. There were also signs the government and military were beginning to appreciate the team's value. The Snowbirds were made an official team, with pilots and groundcrew assigned for the full year. The team was brought back up to nine-plane strength, just in time for its international debut in the United States.

In the following year, the team came into its own. Pilot competitions were opened to personnel from all Canadian military bases; a spring training camp was established in Comox, British Columbia to help acquaint team members with difficult terrain; and the team began the practice of taking off and landing all nine aircraft in close formation. It was a subtle but impressive display of their increasing skill and confidence.

1974 was an exciting season for audiences too. The Snowbirds had attained full aerobatic status, and the Tutors had been given a fresh red, white and blue paint scheme. Early in the season, the

"He was a professional pilot in that he lived to fly and flew to live. His thirst to be airborne was only exceeded by the comradeship he offered to his fellowman."

team made history by becoming the first North American formation flying team to perform north of the Arctic Circle, at Inuvik, North West Territories. A year later, they logged another first by performing under the midnight sun at Inuvik.

The team was still operating from year to year, but hope for permanent status was kindled when they were made a separate unit of the Canadian Forces at CFB Moose Jaw. The Snowbirds had now matched the Golden Hawks five-year life span.

Since their first performance, the Snowbirds had been gradually gaining international fame. Two events in 1976 helped solidify this reputation. First, they were invited to perform at a major American Bicentennial event in Philadelphia on July 4th. They flew the Liberty Bell formation, created especially for the occasion. Second, they were asked to be a part of the opening ceremonies for the 1976 Summer Olympics in Montreal, an event televised world-wide.

Original paint scheme was predominantly white with some red on the nose, tail and smoke tanks. In 1974, a new paint scheme introduced the now-familiar red, white and blue colours.

erhaps these successes played a role in the Snowbirds designation, in 1977, as the Canadian Forces Air Demonstration Team, CFADT, a permanent unit of the Canadian Forces. It was a major step forward. Then in April of 1978, the team was granted permanent squadron status. It was the realization of a dream, and a major achievement. Never before had a Canadian military aerobatic team been given squadron status. The Snowbirds had arrived.

As Canadian Forces 431 Air Demonstration Squadron, the Snowbirds inherited a proud history. The original 431 was formed in England on November 11th, 1942. It won battle honours during the height of World War II, flying strategic and tactical bombing missions over Europe. After the surrender of the Nazis, the Squadron was reassigned to the Pacific theatre. The sudden end of the war, however, led instead to the Squadron's disbandment at Dartmouth, Nova Scotia in 1945.

Thirty-three years later, the Snowbirds proudly assumed the motto of the 431 Iroquois Squadron: *"The Hatiten Ronteriios", Warriors of the Air.*

The 1978 show season had barely started when Capt Gordon de Jong, a second year veteran of the team, was killed during a show in Grande Prairie, Alberta. Capt de Jong was pulling out of a solo manoeuvre when structural failure caused his aircraft to break up in flight. He ejected seconds before the plane crashed to the ground, but was fatally injured.

"Gord was doing what he loved to do," the Snowbirds said in a published memorial, "and he was doing it as well as it could be done when he died. His death cannot take away the example of his courage and his friendship."

Following the accident, there were questions as to whether the Snowbirds would fly at all in 1978. For the pilots and groundcrew, however, there was no doubt. After memorial services and time to regroup, the Snowbirds once again took to the skies.

Through the 1980s, the team developed new formations to add to their repertoire, including crowd-pleasing nine-plane formations at the open and close of each show. The team was asked to perform at more high profile events, such as the Canadian Constitution Repatriation Ceremony in Ottawa in 1982, the Opening Ceremonies of the Universiade Games in Edmonton in 1983, and celebrations for the 75th Anniversary of Powered Flight in Canada and 60th Anniversary of the Royal Canadian Air Force in 1984. These appearances established the Snowbirds as a symbol of Canadian pride.

The Five Nation Flypast

KATSU TOKUNAGA

In honour of Expo '86, Snowbird #1 led an international flypast at the 1986 Abbotsford Airshow. From upper left: *Blue Angels*, United States; *Frecce Tricolori*, Italy; *Snowbirds*, Canada; *Patrouille de France*, France; *Esquadrilha da Fumaca*, Brazil.

"It was a real honour and a great challenge," says LCol (ret) Yogi Huyghebaert, then Snowbird Team Lead.

"The Canadian, French and Italian aircraft were compatible, but the Brazilian aircraft had a top speed of 210 knots, while the U.S. Navy aircraft had his flaps manoeuvring at about 200 knots. We flew a VIC formation with the Brazilian aircraft on the right side and the U.S. Navy aircraft on the outside left, and made all turns to the right to allow the slower aircraft the inside of the turn. It was a memorable experience."

At the same time, the team was growing in popularity south of the border. On July 4th, 1986, they performed before their largest one-day audience ever: one million people at Coney Island, New York.

The team returned home to fly several memorable performances at Expo '86 in Vancouver. Later that summer at the annual

To millions of Canadians, the Snowbirds are a symbol of our nation, something we can call our own. It doesn't matter if you live in Inuvik, NWT or Gander, NFLD, in Sept-Iles, QUE or Victoria, BC - when the Snowbirds soar across the sky, we all share in the excitement ... and the pride.

Abbotsford Airshow, Snowbird #1 lead a historic five-plane flypast with teams from Europe, South America, and the United States.

The team collected its second major honour, the Art Scholl Memorial Showmanship Award, in 1987. The first was the Spirit of Flight Award from the Aviation Hall of Fame bestowed in 1985. The Art Scholl Award was given by the International Council of Airshows in Las Vegas, Nevada. It acknowledged the airshow act which best exemplified qualities demonstrated by Art Scholl, an aerobatic pilot known for showmanship and choreography.

The highlight of the 1988 season was a rare February performance at the Opening Ceremonies of the Winter Olympics in Calgary. To mark the occasion, all nine aircraft trailed coloured smoke – a first in Snowbirds history. With an estimated television audience of over two billion, the performance gave the whole world a look at Canada's Snowbirds.

The season came to an early and tragic end in September when a motor vehicle accident claimed the life of Capt Wes Mackay, Snowbird Lead Solo, and badly injured Capt Paul Giles, Inner Right Wing, and Capt Ken Rae, Opposing Solo.

A memorial plaque in the Snowbirds lounge, donated by the groundcrew, was inscribed with these words: *"With the advent of another year, the performances will go on. But the memory of the professionalism and devotion of Capt Mackay will continue to live on in each and every one of us."*

The 1989 season began on schedule with nine aircraft. Then, almost a year to the day of Capt Mackay's death, tragedy struck again. The team was performing the seven-plane Upward-Downward Bomb Burst manoeuvre at the CNE in Toronto. Capt Shane Antaya, Inner Right Wing, brushed the wingtip of Team Lead, Major Dan Dempsey.

The crowd watched in horror as both planes went out of control. Major Dempsey managed to eject seconds before his aircraft exploded into a ball of flame. Capt Antaya, 26, was killed when his aircraft crashed into Lake Ontario.

On their return home to CFB Moose Jaw, Major Dempsey led the team in the Missing Man formation. When asked by the press if the Snowbirds would fly their remaining shows, he said "every member of this team is a volunteer, and we feel strongly about what we do. Our top priority right now is to take care of Shane and his family, but then we'll take care of the Snowbirds."

The team missed eight shows, but returned to fly the remaining six of the 1989 season.

When the Snowbirds celebrated their 20th Anniversary in 1990, letters of congratulation poured in from around the world. The team received an Air Force Commendation, and marked their milestone 1000th show at CFB Edmonton by introducing red smoke to the display, as well as several new manoeuvres. The Maple Leaf Burst commemorated the Silver Anniversary of the Canadian Flag. The Philion Roll honoured the courage of burn victim Joey Philion, and was an example of the Snowbirds ongoing connection to the hearts and minds of the Canadian public.

In 1991, the team created a sensation during a brief "cameo" appearance with the U.S. Navy Blue Angels at Disney World's 20th anniversary celebrations in Florida, and made the front page of the Sunday New York Times with a flight over the Statue of Liberty.

At home, crowds responded enthusiastically to Snowbirds flypasts at the Molson Indy in Toronto, the Grey Cup in Winnipeg and Canada Day in Ottawa. The team was honoured to serve as official ambassadors of Canada 125 in 1992, performing before some 3.5 million spectators at shows across the continent. In 1993, the team again made history when it became the first Canadian aerobatics team to perform in Mexico.

By the end of 1995, their 25th year, the Snowbirds will have been seen by more than 80 million people. Their survival through the years is a testament to the determination, talent and tenacity of every team member. They are Canada's Snowbirds – a proud symbol of our nation, and a true reflection of the calibre of the men and women of the Canadian Forces.

Wingtip
to
Wingtip

Snowbirds Pilots

Ask any team member, past or present, what they thought of being a Snowbird, and you will invariably get a response that goes something like, "it's the best job you could ever have."

Forget the months of intensive practice, the long separations from family, the physical strain of aerobatic flying, even the danger ... it's all part of the price you pay for being a member of Canada's 431 Air Demonstration Squadron, the Snowbirds. The fact that pilots stand in line to compete for a spot on the team is a real tribute, not only to the Snowbirds, but to the men and women of the Canadian Forces.

The November Tryouts

Every Snowbirds pilot earns their place on the team. The Squadron Commander (also known as Snowbird #1, Team Lead, or the Boss) is appointed, but the candidate must be an officer with the rank of Major who has had a previous tour as a Snowbird. The Team Lead oversees the selection process for Snowbirds #10 and #11, Coordinators, and is consulted regarding the selection of Snowbird #12, Logistics Officer.

The pilots, Snowbirds #2 through #9, earn their spots on the team by demonstrating their skill in flying competitions held in the fall. Being a Snowbird is a two-year tour of duty, so about half the team's roster changes every year.

The tryouts are open to pilots from military bases across Canada. To qualify, a pilot must have at least 1300 hours flying time, excellent flying skills, and the ability to perform well under pressure. Only eight candidates are selected for the two week fly-off.

The actual competition is intense. The candidates do not perform aerobatics, but instead show off their mastery of basic flying skills in thirteen flights, including a solo demonstration, formation demonstration, solo assessment flight, two and four-plane formations and solo manoeuvres. Second year Snowbirds judge their performance. It's the best possible introduction to the Snowbirds' style of flying, because it emphasizes precision and smoothness.

JOHN McQUARRIE

A crewman helps his pilot strap in. The friendships that develop between Snowbirds pilots and groundcrew transcend rank ... and often last a lifetime.

RUSS HEINL

"Taking off and landing in nine-plane formation is recognized as unique to the Snowbirds," says Maj Bob Stephan, Team Lead (91-92).

The working day usually begins with a thorough weather briefing and flight briefing. The pilots then take to the air to show their stuff. This is where the competition really heats up. Even small errors, like being a few seconds off on a roll, can cost you a chance at making the team.

Another kind of assessment takes place on the ground. At briefing and debriefing sessions and afterhours social events, Snowbirds and candidates get to know each other. It's a crucial part of the selection process. Team members must get along well, because personality conflicts between individuals can affect the team's performance in the air.

The final selection of four pilots as new Snowbirds is an emotional time. "You know at the beginning of tryouts that only four will be selected," says LCol (ret) Yogi Huyghebaert, Team Lead 1985-86, "but when you're dealing with eight very good officer/pilots, it's extremely hard to tell four of them that they didn't make the team."

When the choices have been made, the new Snowbirds are assigned their position. Snowbirds #2 and #3 are Inners; Snowbirds #4 and #5 are Line Asterns, Snowbirds #6 and #7 are Outers, and Snowbirds #8 and #9 are Solos. Each position on the team requires a unique set of skills.

Snowbirds #1 through #7 keep their position for the entire two-year tour. Solos advance from Opposing Solo in their first year to Lead Solo in their second.

Practice, Practice, Practice

Training begins almost as soon as tryouts are finished. The team has only four months to get ready for the show season, and they make use of every hour.

The first briefing of the day usually begins at 0830 hours (that's 8:30am in civilian time), depending on sunrise times. The Team Lead prepares the team for the morning training flight, which lasts about an hour and is followed by a debriefing session around 1100 hours. This session is often tougher than the flight itself, especially for first year team members. Every miscue is pointed out by fellow pilots, and videos of the flight are scrutinized for the smallest of errors. For a Snowbird pilot, anything less than their best effort is unacceptable – to themselves and the team.

About 1230 hours, the process begins again with an afternoon briefing, followed by another flight and debriefing. When training is over for the day, pilots take care of other duties, such as maintaining their Instrument Rating, ensuring personal safety equipment is serviceable, keeping log entries up-to-date, and carrying out public relations duties.

Learning to fly in perfect unison takes months of practice. New Snowbirds need about 200 hours of tight formation flying before they are considered ready for the show season. At the start of training in December, the formations are loose. This means there's quite a bit of space between each aircraft, and manoeuvres are performed at higher altitudes. By the end of the spring training session in Comox, British Columbia, however, the team is flying Snowbirds' style – 4 feet of wing overlap and 3-4 feet of vertical separation between each aircraft, at a show altitude of 350 feet above the ground.

JERRY DAVIDSON

Team Lead

The Squadron Commander is Snowbird #1, Team Lead. Flying front and centre, Team Lead calls the formations, which spectators on the ground hear over the PA system, such as "Big Diamond, Go." More important, though, Snowbird #1 sets the pace for each formation: how fast, how high, how steep. It's a position that requires equal measures of experience, intelligence and courage.

"You're the eyes of the team," says Maj Bob Stephan, Team Lead (1991-92), Solo (1989, 1983-84). "Everyone is following you, so you've got to fly as smoothly as you can, as accurately as you can, as predictably as you can. It's totally different than flying Solo, where you have to be more aggressive. Every show is different: the terrain, wind, weather - nothing is ever the same twice. That makes it a challenge, but when you're lucky enough to be chosen Snowbirds Team Lead, it's a challenge you look forward to."

The Inners

Smooth is the key word for Snowbirds #2 and #3, Inner Right Wing and Inner Left Wing, respectively. These pilots fly on either side and just behind #1, Team Lead, and have the task of translating the Lead's intentions to other team members. If an error is made, the Inners have to spot it quickly – but correct it slowly.

Explains Capt Ross Granley, Inner Right (1990-91), "the Inners have to work at not letting themselves get pushed around. If you get too close to #1, Team Lead, the airflow will suck you in even tighter; if you get too far away, the airflow tends to push you out even more. When it happens, you have to be alert enough to recognize the error, but disciplined enough to let the guys flying off you correct first, then slowly correct back to your position. If you correct too quickly, the guys flying off you can't fly smoothly."

16

Line Asterns

Snowbird #4, First Line Astern and Snowbird #5, Second Line Astern fly directly behind the Team Lead to form the "stem" of many formations. Snowbird #4 is a little smoother, Snowbird #5 a little more aggressive, but the defining skill for both is their ability to think and act quickly.

"Oh my gosh, what have I got myself into?" was the initial reaction of Second Line Astern Don Barnby (1987-88) on his first practice flight. "#5 is at the back of the formation, where there's lots of movement because your windscreen is full of airplanes. It took a lot of practice to learn the position, but not so long for me to appreciate the view. That windscreen full of planes was the best sight in the world."

Outers

It takes a certain aggressiveness to be Snowbird #6, Outer Right Wing or Snowbird #7, Outer Left Wing. Flying one plane off the Team Lead, the Outers must be able to see and correct errors quickly in order to stay in formation. Even small miscues are visible from the ground.

"Flying Outer is more difficult physically, I think, while flying Inner is more difficult mentally," says Larry Currie, who flew Outer Right in 1972 and Inner Right in 1973. "The year I changed was one of the first times we tried to move from one position to another. It was a tough adjustment, and we tried to make that experience known. That's one of the reasons the team positions stay the same for the two-year tour."

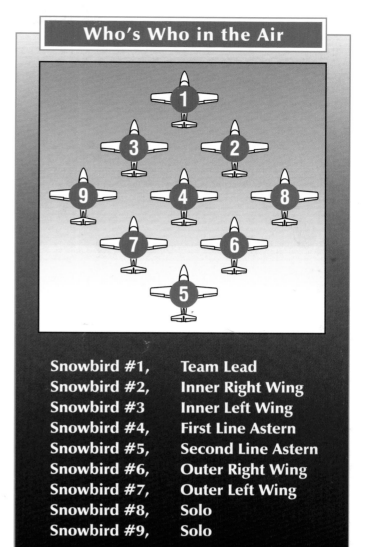

Who's Who in the Air

Snowbird #1,	Team Lead
Snowbird #2,	Inner Right Wing
Snowbird #3	Inner Left Wing
Snowbird #4,	First Line Astern
Snowbird #5,	Second Line Astern
Snowbird #6,	Outer Right Wing
Snowbird #7,	Outer Left Wing
Snowbird #8,	Solo
Snowbird #9,	Solo

The Big Arrow is one of several nine-plane formations the Snowbirds perform for their fans.

Solos

Snowbird #8 and Snowbird #9 are the Solos. The first year is the Opposing Solo, the second year veteran is the Lead Solo. In 9-plane formations they take up outer wing positions. Their finesse and keen sense of timing on daring head-on passes adds excitement to every Snowbirds performance.

"It isn't dangerous at all," says Eric (Speedy) Fast, (1976-77) of being a solo, "you know exactly what the other guy is going to do. When you're coming in for a cross-over, you call contact – which means you see the other plane – from about a mile back. If you don't call contact, you break out of the roll. When you do, the cross happens less than a second later."

Coordinators

Snowbirds #10 and #11, Coordinators, are qualified pilots, but they don't perform at airshows - they organize them. That means checking out show sites, meeting with show sponsors and organizers, and arranging schedules. But it doesn't stop there.

"Coordinators also provide commentary during each show," says LCol (ret) Yves Bosse, Coordinator (1978-79). "The practice of providing a bilingual commentary was started in 1978, and I was the first. I also flew formation for a year, as Second Line Astern (1980). That move was exciting, but I did miss the personal side of being a Coordinator, where you get to meet the show organizers and sponsors."

The radical twins, Solos #8 and #9, perform a series of daring head-on passes, cross-overs and rolls in front of the crowd.

Logistics Officer

Snowbird #12, Logistics Officer, is responsible for the day-to-day administration and financial duties required by the Snowbirds. #12 does not travel with the team, but instead holds down the fort at Squadron headquarters at CFB Moose Jaw.

"The Logistics Officer is the focal point of the team in terms of everything that doesn't have to do with flying or maintaining the aircraft," explains Capt Tana Beer, Logistics Officer (1993-95). "You find yourself doing a lot of very different tasks, like representing the Squadron Commander when the team's on the road, or answering some of the 700-1000 fan letters the team gets every year. Everyday is a little different, because something new always seems to crop up ... the job really expands your horizons."

Since 1971, more than 300 men and women have flown with the Snowbirds. Their skill has brought the team national and international recognition, but every pilot seems to know that the team is more than the sum of its parts. "The team's the thing," says one former Snowbird, "you play your part for two years and move on; the team continues. But those two years, they're worth ten lifetimes."

Countdown to show time. "Coordinators arrive at the show site about two hours before the team," says Capt Mike Lenehan, Coordinator #11 (1992-94), "We make sure everything is ready, including fuel for the planes, diesel fuel for smoke, hotel rooms, the final show schedule and so on. At show time, we narrate the performance."

19

CANOPY AND SEAT CATAPULTS
CONTAIN EXPLOSIVE CHARGES
FOR REMOVE
CUT FLEXIBLE HOSES AT DECALS

DANGER

CREW CHIEF - SGT MARK DOANE

R/H

"When your crew puts their stamp of approval

on the aircraft, you know it's safe to fly."

Back on the Ground

Snowbirds Groundcrew

In their twenty-five year history, the Snowbirds have never had to cancel or delay a performance because of a technical malfunction in the aircraft. This sterling record belongs to the highly trained Snowbirds Groundcrew - the other half of 431 Squadron.

twenty-five years

The Snowbirds' spotless attendance record doesn't mean the aircraft never break down, they do. It simply means the groundcrew have always been able to correct problems before show time. Their ability to effect a wide range of repairs using only basic tools is legendary.

"I have nothing but admiration for the groundcrew," says LCol (ret) Yogi Huyghebaert, Team Lead (1985-86) and Solo pilot (1974-75). "These people are so dedicated I have seen them spend half the night working on aircraft to prepare them for the next day's show."

A Unique Brand of Teamwork

Groundcrew earn their position on the Snowbirds through a demonstration of skill, teamwork, and innovative thinking. Team Lead and Crew Chief make the final selections for the team. Successful candidates need to exhibit both physical and mental stamina, because during their two-year assignment they will be asked to provide quick and effective solutions to a wide range of problems.

A typical Snowbirds Groundcrew includes a Crew Chief, Deputy Crew Chief, two Aero-Engine Technicians, two Airframe Technicians, two Instrument Electrical Technicians, one Communications/Radar Technician, one Safety Systems Technician, and one Supply Technician. Their job is to inspect, test, repair and maintain all aircraft systems and components, whether the team is at home or on the road.

Groundcrew are assigned a number from #1A - #12A: #1A is always the Crew Chief, #12A is the

Packing the Tutor for transit. The Snowbirds do not have a transport plane. Instead, each aircraft carries one pilot, one crewman, their luggage, and assorted tools and equipment. It's a tight squeeze.

Supply Technician, but #2A through #11A can refer to any crew member: Deputy Crew Chief, Airframe, Aero-Engine, Instrument Electrical, Communications/Radar or Safety Systems.

Each team member is responsible for aircraft maintenance in his or her specific trade. Each crewman is responsible for the day-to-day maintenance of his or her aircraft. This means keeping it polished on the outside, running at peak efficiency on the inside. There's no room for error: problems must be spotted quickly and corrected immediately.

When the crew puts their stamp of approval on the aircraft, you know it's safe to fly.

One of the things that makes the Snowbirds unique is the way each crewman is partnered with an aircraft and pilot. For Snowbird #2, Inner Right Wing, for example, there is Snowbird #2A, Crewman; #3 is teamed with #3A ... and so on. Snowbird #1, Team Lead is always matched with Snowbird #1A, Crew Chief.

When the team takes off for another show, each Tutor carries pilot and crew. The pair log a lot of hours in the air, so it doesn't take long for the traditional barrier of rank to be replaced by a bond of friendship. It's a true partnership, which is why you see pilots' names emblazoned under the canopy on one side of the aircraft, crewmen's on the other.

Crewmen's Work is Never Done

When the Snowbirds are at home training, a crewman's day typically begins around 0730 hours with a Daily Inspection (called a DI) and a Before Flight Check (B✓). With a final wash of windscreens and canopies, the planes are towed outside and readied for flight.

The crew moves back into action when the team returns. After Flight Checks (A✓) and Quick Turn Around Checks (AB✓) are done on every aircraft, then groundcrew tend to the maintenance requirements of their Tutor. Any snags, or malfunctions, mentioned by the pilot have to be fixed before the afternoon flight. The routine is repeated twice a day, five or six days a week until show season.

During the season, there's only one flight per day, but still not much spare time. Groundcrew are responsible for packing and unpacking the aircraft for the transit to each show site, and keeping them clean and polished for the public. When maintenance problems occur, they must be fixed on the spot with whatever tools and parts are available. It takes innovative thinking to keep Snowbirds' aircraft in top flying condition.

Snowbirds Groundcrew represent a broad range of expertise. Aero-Engine Technicians carry out ground inspections, modifications and adjustments to the propulsion systems, repair or replace worn parts, and perform regular quality assurance checks. Airframe Technicians maintain the craft's airframe and aircraft systems, including landing gear, air conditioning and pressurization systems, the fuel system, and anti-icing/de-icing systems.

Most of the Tutor's systems are easily accessible, but sometimes you just have to crawl in for a closer look.

Instrument Electrical Technicians are responsible for aircraft electrical, electronic and electro-mechanical systems as well as associated components. Communications/Radar Technicians ensure all airborne communications systems – intercom, radio navigation and pulse navigation systems – function properly.

Safety Systems Technicians maintain life preservers, parachutes, ejection seats, escape systems, survival/medical kits, oxygen masks, flying helmets and visors, and oxygen-nitrogen systems in top working order. The Supply Technician does not travel with the team, but stays in Moose Jaw to ensure the day-to-day needs are met, such as getting spare parts shipped to show sites, distributing public relations material, and maintaining control of spare parts and stocks.

Snowbirds Groundcrew set the standard for dedication to one's craft. That dedication, though rarely seen by the public, has made 25 years of Snowbirds air demonstration excellence possible.

RICK RADELL

Dedication

23

RICK MACNAB

Snowbirds flying their trademark 9-plane Big Diamond formation with "Smoke On". Low grade diesel fuel makes the best smoke, according to 1989-90 Crew Chief Dan Bergeron. "I remember one show site where we found some of the ugliest, dirtiest fuel you can imagine. It was 15 years old and good for nothing else, but we took it. And you know, it made great smoke."

"Smoke On"

When the Team Lead calls "Smoke On" over the radio, each pilot turns the switch and planes begin trailing red and white smoke. Red smoke was introduced to Snowbirds displays in 1990, when WO Dan Bergeron was #1A, Crew Chief. Bergeron had been to England that winter to learn how Britain's Red Arrows aerobatics team made their red smoke displays.

"The problem for us was getting the right colour mix and the right delivery system for the Tutor. Our first attempts during the winter created more of a pinkish smoke, but after much trial and error, we got red smoke.

"We almost didn't use the coloured smoke," he adds, "because we couldn't find a way to clean the aircraft. With the Tutors, the smoke system is all external, so a lot of colour gets on the underside of the plane. We tried every kind of solvent with no luck. Then we tried cream soap, the kind mechanics use to clean their hands, and it worked, so the Snowbirds had red smoke."

JERRY DAVIDSON

"Being the first woman on the groundcrew wasn't the most important thing to me," says Cpl Marlene Shillingford, Snowbird #7A, Airframe (93-94), "I joined the Snowbirds because it was something I'd always dreamed of doing. And it was a great experience, especially getting to fly with the team on transits between show sites. That, the friendships, and being an ambassador for Canada were the best parts of being a Snowbird."

Aerobatics are hard on aircraft. Keeping the Snowbirds' Tutors in top flying condition is the responsibility — and pride — of the groundcrew.

Groundcrew Check List

What does it take to keep the Snowbirds flying high? Many hours of hard work on the ground. Crew members are responsible for inspecting their own aircraft with respect to all technical points. Here's an overview of a typical B✓, or Before Flight Check and an A✓, or After Flight Check.

BEFORE FLIGHT CHECK

AIRFRAME

Visually inspect exterior of aircraft
Check hydraulic and brake reservoirs
Visually check fuel level including external tanks if installed
Visually inspect windshield and canopy assemblies
Visually inspect cockpit; ensure article security
Ensure landing gear emergency handle is in FULL position
Visually inspect tires; ensure correct extension on shock struts; ensure nose toggle link pin is secure

AERO-ENGINE

Check jet pipe interior for foreign object damage (FOD)
Check air intake ducts and surrounding area for FOD

INSTRUMENT/ELECTRICAL

Visually inspect all instruments, circuit breakers, lighting panels and switches
Visually inspect witness wire on external tank and switch on tanker aircraft
Visually inspect pitot head and boom for alignment; ensure openings are clear of obstructions
Visually inspect lift transducer
Prior to night flying, visually and functionally check all interior and exterior lighting

SAFETY SYSTEMS

Check oxygen system quantity
Ensure external canopy jettison door is closed and secure

AFTER FLIGHT CHECK

AIRFRAME

Visually inspect exterior of aircraft
Visually inspect windshield and canopy assemblies
Visually inspect cockpit
Ensure landing gear emergency handle is in FULL position
Visually inspect landing gear and gear mechanism
Visually inspect landing gear doors and door mechanism
Visually inspect tires, wheels, brakes and brake lines

AERO-ENGINE

Visually inspect jet pipe assembly, jet pipe retaining ring
Visually inspect jet pipe forward section
Visually inspect intake ducts
Visually inspect jet pipe alignment turnbuckle brackets

INSTRUMENT/ELECTRICAL

Visually inspect all instruments, circuit breakers, lighting panels and switches
Read accelerometer: if pointer is in yellow range, reset; if pointer is at or over red range, record as an over-stress. Ensure locking bar is secured
Visually inspect pitot head and boom for alignment; ensure openings are clear of obstructions
Visually inspect lift transducer

SAFETY SYSTEMS

Install internal canopy jettison initiator pin
Check oxygen system quantity
Ensure oxygen regulator toggles are in NORMAL position and oxygen hoses are correctly stowed

A Canadian Classic

The CT114 Tutor

In its quarter century of service with the Snowbirds, the Tutor jet has earned a special place in the hearts of team members and fans. It has been called "a tough little jet", "beautifully behaved", and "a delight to fly".

twenty-five years

RICK RADELL.

The Tutor-Snowbirds partnership has lasted longer than any other aircraft-aerobatic team pairing in the world. It has been a successful pairing, and it looks as if the Tutor will take the Snowbirds into the next century.

A swept Delta formation flypast over Snowbird #10.

Made in Canada

In the 1950s, the RCAF was shopping around for a single engine, two-seat basic jet trainer to replace the old Harvard trainers. Likely candidates included the British-made Hunting Jet Provost, the American Cessna T-37, and the French CM 170 Fouga Magister. Then there was the underdog, the CL-41 Tutor.

The Tutor was designed and built by Canadair, a private aeronautics company based in Montreal, Quebec. So confident was Canadair in the small jet's capabilities, they went ahead and developed a prototype with private funding.

Test flights began in January of 1960. By December of that year, the RCAF was test flying the prototype. Canadair's confidence in the jet finally paid off in September of 1961, when the RCAF ordered the first of 190 Tutor jet trainers. The last Tutor was built in 1967.

For almost 30 years, all Canadian military pilots have received their flight training on a Tutor.

CAE Aviation modify and maintain the Tutor and Snowbirds' aircraft at their facilities in Edmonton, Alberta.

4.02 m
(13'-2")

4.14 m
(13'-7")

CAF   163

11.12 m
(36'-6")

9.75 m
(32'-0")

2.82 m
(9'-3")

Canada   [1]
Snowbirds   114078

3.6 m
(11'-1")

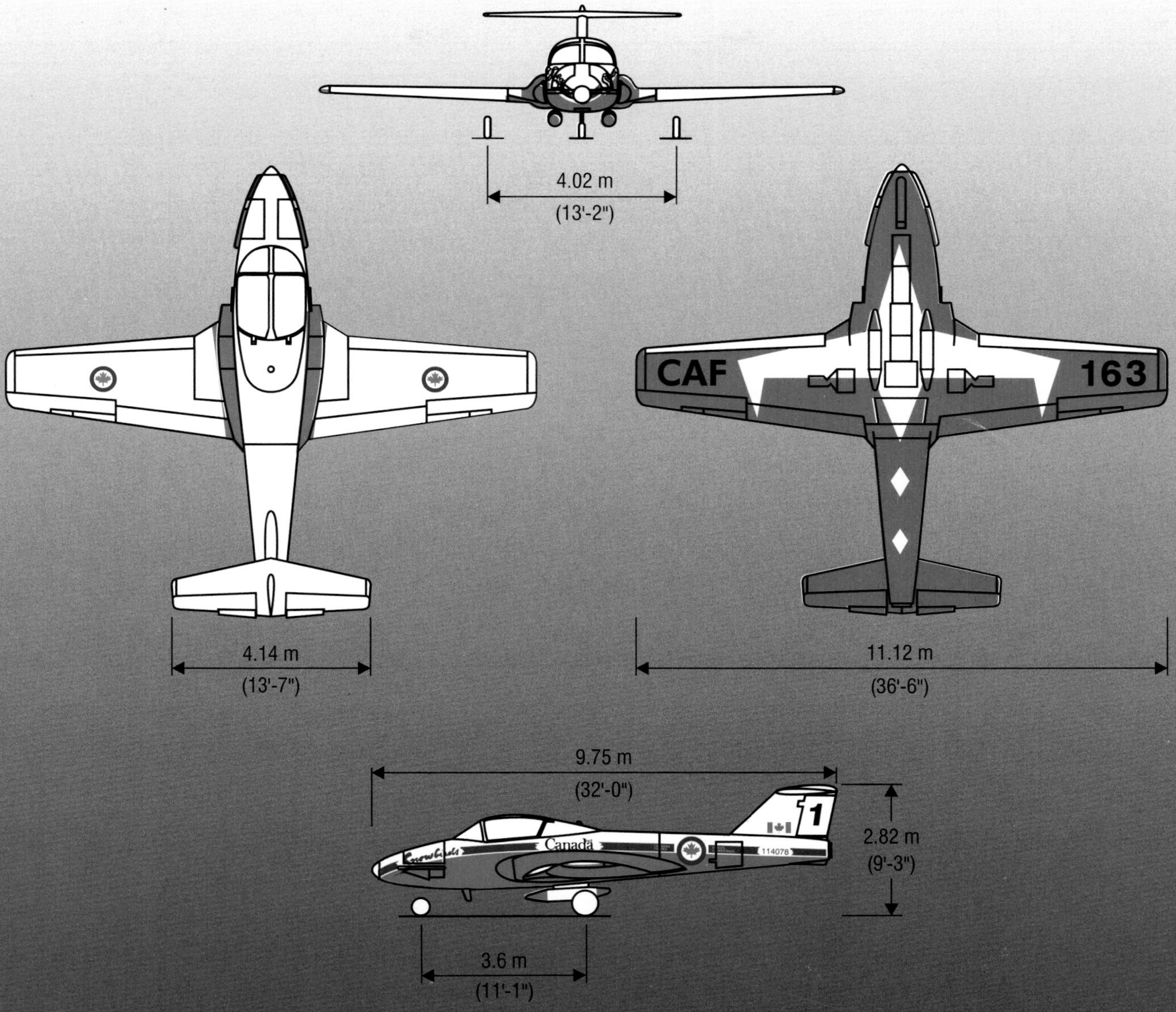

Weight and performance figures for Snowbirds Tutors are slightly different than for school Tutors.

DIMENSIONS

Wing Span	11.12 m (36'6")
Length Overall	9.75 m (32'0")
Height Overall	2.82 m (9'3")
Wheel Track	4.02 m (13'2")

ENGINE

General Electric J85-CAN-40 2-stage turbine with single-spool, 8-stage, axial flow compressor

Length	1.03 m (40.5")
Diametre	0.45 m (17.7")
Weight	172.4 kg (380 lb)

2700 lbs static thrust at sea level
(modified Snowbird aircraft)

WEIGHTS

Empty	2268 kg (5000 lb)
Maximum Take-off Weight	3856 kg (8500 lb)
Maximum Landing Weight	3765 kg (8300 lb)

PERFORMANCE

Service Ceiling	12497 m (41,000 ft)
Maximum speed	428 knots
Minimum speed	90 knots
Rate of climb	152-1829 m (500-6,000 ft)/minute
Cruising speed: 95% rpm at 30,000 ft	340 knots
Range with Fuel Reserve	580 nautical miles or 700 statute miles
Endurance at 35,000 ft	2 hours
g Limits:	- 3 to +7.33 g

Like Snowbirds pilots and groundcrew, the Tutor serves a limited tour of duty with the team. Aerobatic flying is hard on the aircraft, and after their tour they are rotated out to less strenuous duty.

Aerobatic Modifications

There are thirteen Tutors in the Snowbirds' fleet. Eleven travel with the team, while two remain at CFB Moose Jaw as spares. All have been modified for aerobatic use. The most important change is the cross-cockpit modification, which involves installation of a second gear handle and switches for landing and taxi lights, pilot heat and windscreen de-mist on the right side of the aircraft. This allows the Snowbirds' Tutor to be flown solo from either the left or right seat. School Tutors are flown solo from the left seat only.

The other major difference in Snowbirds Tutors are the external smoke tanks. All but two of the Snowbirds are equipped with two smoke tanks. Each contains about 36 gallons of diesel fuel, just enough for one airshow. At the Team Lead's command, the pilot will flip a cockpit switch to initiate smoke. When he does, fuel is pumped from the tank to the rear of the aircraft, where it is sprayed into the jet exhaust and vapourized. This produces a billowing trail of white smoke. The addition of red smoke in 1990 delighted both audiences and photographers.

Maintenance

Like every other member of the Snowbirds, the Tutor serves a tour of duty. After that tour is over, the aircraft is returned to Training Command for less strenuous assignment. The reason for this rotation is physical exhaustion.

Formation aerobatics and solo manoeuvres are tough on the aircraft. Snowbirds' jets can experience fatigue damage at a rate 5 to 25 times faster than school aircraft.

To counter this strain, groundcrew work year-round to keep the aircraft in top flying condition. In addition to daily maintenance, the engine is overhauled every 200 hours flying time, and the whole aircraft is given a thorough inspection every 400 hours flying time.

Since the versatile little jet became the RCAF's primary trainer, approximately 40 Tutors have been used in aerobatic flying. They have been flown by the Red Knight, the Golden Centenaires, and the Snowbirds.

CT114 Tutor

1 Taxi and ground observer lights
2 Upward ejection seat (2)
3 Jettisonable canopy
4 Fuselage break
5 Speed brake (1 each side)
6 Engine compartment
7 Landing light (1 each side)
8 Personal baggage stowage (1 each side)
9 Oxygen cylinder (1 each side)
10 Engine air intake (1 each side)
11 Battery (1 each side)
12 Electrical relay panel (1 each side)
13 Electronic equipment compartment

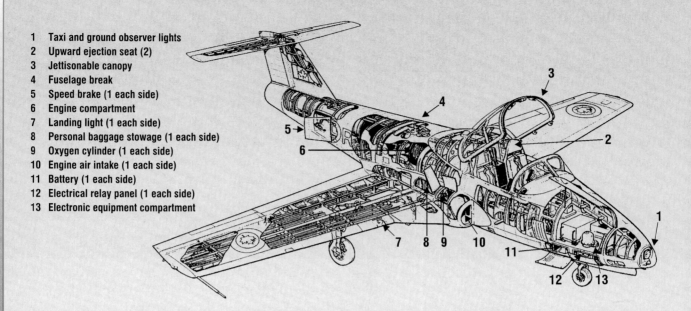

Snowbirds Modified Cockpit

CPL TED DURDIN

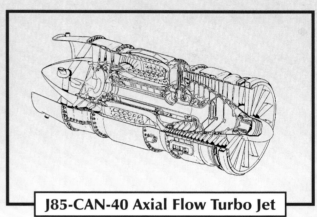

J85-CAN-40 Axial Flow Turbo Jet

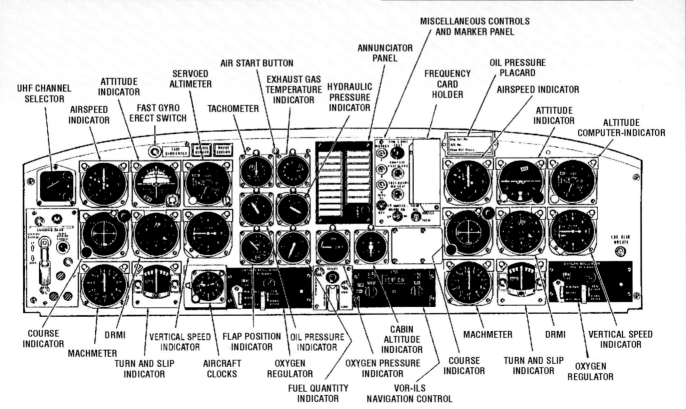

MISCELLANEOUS CONTROLS
AND MARKER PANEL

ANNUNCIATOR
PANEL

AIR START BUTTON

FREQUENCY
CARD
HOLDER

OIL PRESSURE
PLACARD

SERVOED
ALTIMETER

EXHAUST GAS
TEMPERATURE
INDICATOR

HYDRAULIC
PRESSURE
INDICATOR

AIRSPEED INDICATOR

ATTITUDE
INDICATOR

UHF CHANNEL
SELECTOR

ATTITUDE
INDICATOR

TACHOMETER

ALTITUDE
COMPUTER-INDICATOR

AIRSPEED
INDICATOR

FAST GYRO
ERECT SWITCH

COURSE
INDICATOR

DRMI

VERTICAL SPEED
INDICATOR

FLAP POSITION
INDICATOR

OIL PRESSURE
INDICATOR

CABIN
ALTITUDE
INDICATOR

MACHMETER

DRMI

VERTICAL SPEED
INDICATOR

MACHMETER

TURN AND SLIP
INDICATOR

AIRCRAFT
CLOCKS

OXYGEN
REGULATOR

OXYGEN PRESSURE
INDICATOR

COURSE
INDICATOR

TURN AND SLIP
INDICATOR

OXYGEN
REGULATOR

FUEL QUANTITY
INDICATOR

VOR-ILS
NAVIGATION CONTROL

31

Big Diamond, Go!

Formation Flying Snowbirds' Style

When the Snowbirds first began performing in 1971 they were restricted to formation flying – no aerobatics. And yet they thrilled spectators with their tight formations, each one so perfectly timed that from the ground it looked as if seven aircraft were flying as one. By the time aerobatics were added to the show, the Snowbirds were being hailed as one of the world's best air demonstration teams.

twenty-five years

The Big Diamond is flown with 4 feet of wing overlap and 3 feet vertical distance between aircraft. The vertical distance is called flying "metal to metal".

The Snowbirds take off in Big Diamond formation, smoke on. Not every show starts this way; winds must be favourable and the runway wide enough to accommodate wingtip spacing (no wing overlap).

"People on the ground don't realize it, but there's lots of movement in the air," says First Line Astern Vince Jandrisch (1990-91). "My first year was especially bumpy. I remember one show in Edmonton, when I was still new at the game: there was quite a bit of turbulence and on one formation I got too close to the Lead and the airflow from his plane sucked me in. I corrected too quickly and the whole formation bounced around a bit. That's what you learn not to do."

BOB McINTYRE

Without the solos, the Big Diamond turns into the 7-plane Double Diamond, one of the team's tightest formations. "We flew with about 8 feet of wing overlap on that formation," says Second Line Astern Don Barnby (1987-88). "Now when I see it on video, it's hard to believe it's me in one of those planes."

ED DRADER

ED DRADER

ED DRADER

The spectacular Canada Burst fills the sky with billowing smoke trails.

Snowbirds break away during a Downward Bomb Burst. Rejoining after the manoeuvre is an exercise in efficiency. During winter practice sessions the rejoin is rehearsed over and over, until each pilot in the formation knows exactly what to do and where to look to bring the formation smoothly back together.

The 7-plane Mini Concorde (main), and the 9-plane Concorde (inset) with Solos taking the outer left and right positions. From the ground, Snowbirds' formations seem to glide effortlessly across the sky. It's a different story in the air.

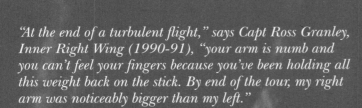

"At the end of a turbulent flight," says Capt Ross Granley, Inner Right Wing (1990-91), "your arm is numb and you can't feel your fingers because you've been holding all this weight back on the stick. By end of the tour, my right arm was noticeably bigger than my left."

ED DRADER

In the Card Nine formation, the pilots are not flying at the same altitude, but on three separate vertical planes. The second line flies about 4 to 6 feet below the first line; the third line about 4 to 6 feet below the second. The separation is necessary because aircraft cannot fly in the exhaust, or wash, of another aircraft. Also, the vertical distance enables the team to present a tighter formation to spectators on the ground.

BILL JOHNSON

It's up to Snowbirds Team Lead to set the profile (rate of roll, speed, altitude, etc) for each formation, such as this Big Arrow. "Having been an Outer has made the transition to Team Lead easier for me," says Maj Steve Hill, Team Lead (1995-96) and Outer Right Wing (1985-86), "because I understand the type of profile the Lead has to set in order for everyone to stay together. You have to get the profile down perfectly each time, while keeping in mind wind and weather conditions, altitude and show line. Putting it all together is a real challenge."

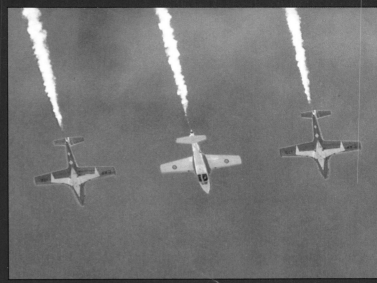

A 3-plane Mirror Pass, often called the Flip-Flop. The lead pilot is inverted as the formation passes show centre. Pilots can fly inverted for only 30 seconds before running out of fuel, so passes are executed quickly and neatly.

The 5-plane Line Abreast formation curves upward into a graceful roll and loop, a manoeuvre that stretches Snowbirds pilots and their Tutor aircraft to the limit.

The 4-plane Double Take changes 180 degrees as it passes in front of the crowd. Look once, Lead #1 and First Line Astern #4 are inverted; look again, Inners #2 and #3 are inverted.

"The Line Abreast roll (left) was the most difficult manoeuvre, especially for the Outers," says Outer Right Wing Dale Hackett (1989-90). "We're flying on the far left and right side of the line. At the top of the roll, I'm on full throttle trying to keep up speed, but #7 [Outer Left Wing] is on idle with his speed brakes on. Then in a split second everything changes: Outer Left is on full throttle and I'm on idle. The physical strain, especially the sudden change in gs, is incredible."

RUSS HEINL

RUSS HEINL

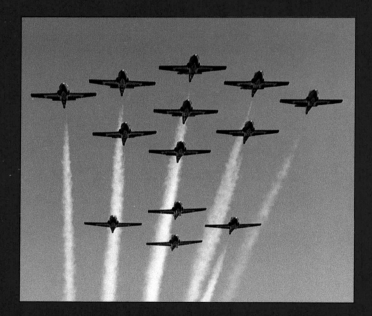

Above, a rare shot showing all 13 Tutors in the Snowbirds fleet: the 9-plane formation and 2 coordinators' aircraft, and 2 spares. Here, Maj Bob Stephan leads the Big Diamond formation on the team's return home to Moose Jaw after the last show of 1991. Following in the box formation are the Coordinators, Maj Real Turgeon and Capt Jeff Hill in Snowbirds #10 and #11, and Capt Mike Lenehan (incoming Coordinator) and LCol (ret) Yogi Huyghebaert (Team Lead 85-86) flying Snowbirds spares.

The Big Diamond (top) and the Concorde (right), show the Snowbirds in two of their most popular 9-plane formations.

RAFE TOMSETT

Solo manoeuvres are real crowd-pleasers. "One of the jobs of the solos," says Solo Rich Lancaster (1990-91), "is to maintain a flying display in front of the crowd at show centre. The breaks between formations are short, maybe 15 seconds or so, but the solos fill them with head-on passes and cross-overs – manoeuvres that get the crowd excited."

The head-on Solo Cross (top) is one of the most exciting manoeuvres. Entering stage left and stage right, Solos #8 and #9 race towards each other at 300 knots, or a closing speed of 600 knots. They call "contact" from a mile back, then cross at show centre less than a second later. At the cross, a wingspan (30 to 50 ft) separates the planes.

The Solo Mirror (top right) gives the illusion of one aircraft and its mirror image. The illusion, which can only be seen at one point along the show line, is fleeting but impressive.

The Dirty Roll (centre right) is a low speed (160 knots) pass that takes its name from a pilot term. Dirty refers to aircraft configuration: landing gear and flaps down, speed brakes out. Clean means landing gear and flaps up, speed brakes in.

At crowd level, the Solo Cross (bottom right) looks like a collision about to happen ... but the skill and timing of the pilots ensures the manoeuvre is safe.

RICK RADELL

RAFE TOMSETT

41

"For me, two of the most important symbols

binding Canada together are our Flag and

our Snowbirds."

Honourary Colonel Fred Sutherland

Goodwill Ambassadors
Proudly Canadian

Over the years, the Snowbirds have received hundreds of letters of appreciation from people of all ages, as well as from all ten Canadian provinces and both territories, twenty-four U.S. states, and as far away as Great Britain, Europe, Australia, and Japan.

Their skill as precision formation fliers has earned the team a place on the world stage. World-wide mass media coverage of their performances at the 1976 Summer Olympics in Montreal and 1988 Winter Olympics in Calgary have made the Snowbirds a recognized Canadian symbol at home and abroad.

The Snowbirds are Goodwill Ambassadors for Canada. After every show, no matter how tired, Snowbirds pilots stand at the crowd line, talking and signing autographs. One man from California wrote, "people here cannot get over what great ambassadors each and every member of your team are. If your mission is to enhance the image of the Canadian Armed Forces and the country of Canada, you guys do a good job!"

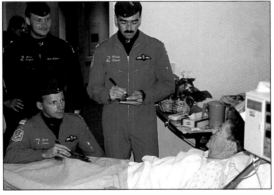

The Snowbirds are serious about their image as Canadian Ambassadors, and provide positive role models for young people.

Why All The Publicity?

Some of the Snowbirds' greatest fans are children. In 1992, the team decided to use this popularity to promote the Fly High Without Drugs campaign. Through posters, televised public service announcements, and personal appearances, the Snowbirds help provide young people with positive role models.

They lend their support to many other charitable organizations, and spend hours visiting schools, hospitals and communities. The team recently became the first Ambassadors for the Canadian Injury Prevention Association, a non-profit charitable group committed to making smart risk-taking and injury prevention a social movement.

"It is an honour to have the Snowbirds as our Ambassadors," says Dr. Conn, Executive Director of the CIPF. "They are perfect role models: they undergo training, wear safety gear, buckle up, drive sober and look first."

Just one more reason why, when the Snowbirds fly, we all feel the pride.

twenty-five years

Family Day

Before the show season begins in late April, the Snowbirds hold their annual Family Day. It's an opportunity for team members and their families to get to know each other, enjoy a barbecue and family games ... and to say their good-byes.

"On Family Day, you know your husband is going away," says Micheline Hamel, wife of Capt Mario Hamel, Snowbird #2 1994-95, "getting everyone together makes the day easier for everyone, especially the children."

RUSS HEINL

Home Again
Moose Jaw

D.J. KRAUS

Above: *The Big Diamond formation soars over Moose Jaw, Saskatchewan, home of the Snowbirds for 25 years.*

Below: *A future Snowbird? Maybe someday, but for now this youngster is content to imitate his dad.*

Right: *The Heart formation is dedicated to Snowbirds' family and friends.*

During the May to October season, the Snowbirds fly over 70 shows, and log more than 400 hours of flying time. Their travels may take them from the Yukon Territory to Texas, and from the Maritimes to British Columbia. It's a rigorous schedule, with little time off between performances. By late autumn, after months on the road, pilots and groundcrew are only too glad to return home to a happy reunion of husbands, wives and children.

Home is 15 Wing Moose Jaw in south central Saskatchewan, where flat prairie and open sky provide ideal year-round flying conditions. Pilots have been honing their skills in these skies since 1941. First it was the site of a British Commonwealth Air Training Plan school, then a Royal Canadian Air Force base, and finally the No. 2CFFTS, Canadian Forces Flying Training School known as The Big 2.

BILL JOHNSON

twenty-five years

Hush - The silence lingers still
White clouds brush the distant hill
The Snowbirds flown on silent wings
Far from earth bound, tugging strings.

Hush - There lies but one man sleeping
A date with his Maker he is keeping
Though once he raced across the sky, in flight
Radiant, as a star at night.

Hush - He was an airman bold
Who saw the sunset turning gold
Who soared with grace across this land
A brave man, in a brave man's band.

No more in danger shall he tread
No more the sunsets turning red
Though high above our prairie fleece
We know his soul will find its peace.

Hush - The Snowbird's taken flight
Into the great beyond of night
To join his comrades, in the wing
Which flies just for our Heavenly King.

- *Peter Watt*

The
Last Roll

In Memory of
Fallen Snowbirds

Among the world's air demon-stration teams, the Snowbirds are well-known for their skill, but they are not immune to tragedy. Four Snowbirds pilots have lost their lives in the performance of their duty.

Capt Lloyd Waterer
#8, Lead Solo
Killed during an airshow in
Trenton, Ontario in 1972
Age 24

Capt Gordon de Jong
#8, Lead Solo
Killed during an airshow in
Grande Prairie, Alberta in 1978
Age 32

Capt Wes Mackay
#8, Lead Solo
Killed in a motor vehicle accident
after a performance in
Latrobe, Pennsylvania in 1988
Age 28

Capt Shane Antaya
#2, Inner Right Wing
Killed during an airshow at the CNE in
Toronto, Ontario in 1989
Age 26

These Snowbirds have passed away since completion of their tour: Andy Bissette, #11, Coordinator (1974): John Shaw, #2, Inner Right Wing (1974-75): Jim Sorfleet, #4, First Line Astern (1976-77): Bob Drake, #4, First Line Astern (1980-81): Tristan deKoninck, #4, First Line Astern (1982-83).

Every Snowbirds performance is a tribute to these men ... and to all the men and women of Canadian Forces 431 Air Demonstration Squadron who have dedicated themselves to excellence.

twenty-five years

Roll Call

25 Years of Snowbirds

Skill. Dedication. Excellence. Meet the men and women who have kept the Snowbirds tradition alive for twenty-five years.

1971

AIR CREW: #1 Maj Glen Younghusband (Team Lead), #2 Capt Tom Gernack, #3 Capt Inch Illingsworth, #4 Capt Chester Glendenning, #5 Capt Fred McCague, #6 Capt Gord Wallis, #7 Capt Mike Marynowski, #8 Capt George Hawey, #9 Lt Lloyd Waterer, #10 Capt Bob Sharp, #11 Lt Doug Zebedee

AIR CREW: #1 Maj Glen Younghusband (Team Lead), #2 Capt Tom Gernack, #3 Capt Inch Illingsworth,
#4 Lt Larry Currie, #5 Capt Chester Glendenning, #6 Capt Fred McCague, #7 Capt Gord Wallis, #8 Capt Lloyd Waterer,
#9 Capt Mike Marynowski, #10 Capt John Hackett GROUND CREW: #1A Sgt Bill Holloway (Crew Chief),
#2A MCpl Ron LaGrange, #3A MCpl Larry Legault, #4A Cpl Mike Thompson, #5A Cpl Dwight Vaughn,
#6A Cpl Claude Mikkelson, #7A Cpl Peter Hennicke, #8A Cpl Joe McCluskey, #9A Cpl Bob Nixon, #10A Cpl Reg Bach

AIR CREW: #1 Maj George Miller (Team Lead), #2 Capt Larry Currie, #3 Capt Mike Murphy, #4 Capt Carl Stef,
#5 Lt Bob Wade, #6 Capt George Hawey, #7 Capt Gord Wallis, #8 Capt Tom Griffis, #9 Capt Inch Illingsworth,
#10 Capt John Hackett GROUND CREW: #1A Sgt Bill Holloway (Crew Chief), #2A Cpl John Doerkson,
#3A Cpl Ely Bowen, #4A Cpl Ed Torfason, #5A Cpl Chuck Wicks, #6A Cpl Bob LeBlanc, #7A Cpl Peter Hennicke,
#8A Cpl Claude Mikkelson, #9A MCpl Larry Legault, #10A Cpl Rusty Rutherford

Courtesy: DOUG MARSHALL

AIR CREW: #1 Maj George Miller (Team Lead), #2 Capt John Shaw, #3 Lt Mike Murphy, #4 Capt Carl Stef,
#5 Lt Bob Wade, #6 Capt Murray Bertram, #7 Capt Harry Chapin, #8 Capt Tom Griffis, #9 Capt Yogi Huyghebaert,
#10 Capt Greg Bruneau, #11 Capt Andy Bissette/Capt Mike Savard GROUND CREW: #1A Sgt Doug Marshall
(Crew Chief), #2A Cpl Ray Lund, #3A Cpl Ely Bowen, #4A Cpl Rusty Rutherford, #5A Cpl Al Boyce,
#6A Cpl Mike Thompson, #7A MCpl Cal Wanvig, #8A Cpl Peter Hennicke, #9A Cpl Ed Torfason

1972

1973

1974

1975

AIR CREW: #1 Maj Denis Gauthier (Team Lead), #2 Capt John Shaw, #3 Capt Chris Tuck, #4 Capt Dave Wilson, #5 Capt Carl Stef, #6 Capt Murray Bertram, #7 Capt Harry Chapin, #8 Capt Ken Carr, #9 Capt Yogi Huyghebaert, #10 Capt Greg Bruneau, #11 Capt Jack Girard, #12 Capt Roy Gateley GROUND CREW: #1A Sgt Bill Holloway (Crew Chief, #2A Cpl Ray Lund, #3A Cpl Fred Broderick, #4A Cpl Garth Suitor, #5A Cpl Al Boyce, #6A Cpl Wayne Swayze, #7A MCpl Cal Wanvig, #8A Cpl Peter Hennicke, #9A Cpl Ed Torfason, #10A Cpl Bud Peters

1976

AIR CREW: #1 Maj Denis Gauthier (Team Lead), #2 Capt Gerry Nicks, #3 Capt Chris Tuck, #4 Capt Dave Wilson, #5 Capt Paul Beaulieu, #6 Capt Jim Sorfleet, #7 Capt Harry Chapin, #8 Capt Ken Carr, #9 Capt Eric Fast, #10 Capt Jack Girard, #11 Capt Mike Jephcott, #12 Capt Roy Gateley GROUND CREW: #1A Sgt Doug Marshall (Crew Chief), #2A Cpl John Zorn, #3A Cpl Moe Taylor, #4A Cpl Ross Chapman, #5A Cpl Gary Friesen, #6A MCpl Nick Nichols, #7A Cpl Chuck Wicks, #8A Cpl Vern Opperman, #9A MCpl Cal Wanvig, #10A Cpl Ian Neilson ADMIN: Pte. Raaen

1977

AIR CREW: #1 Maj Gord Wallis (Team Lead), #2 Capt Gerry Nicks, #3 Capt Wayne Thompson, #4 Capt Jim Sorfleet, #5 Capt Joseph Molnar, #6 Capt Keith Coulter, #7 Maj Paul Beaulieu, #8 Capt Gord de Jong, #9 Capt Eric Fast, #10 Capt Mike Jephcott, #11 Capt Stuart Morgan, #12 Capt Jack Girard GROUND CREW: #1A Sgt Harold Breadner (Crew Chief), #2A MCpl Garth Suitor, #3A MCpl Wally Corbin, #4A MCpl Nick Nichols, #5A Cpl Moe Taylor, #6A Cpl Ross Chapman, #7A Cpl Ian Neilson, #8A Cpl John Zorn, #9A Cpl Barry Dickson, #10A Cpl Bob O'Reilly ADMIN: SG Richard (Civilian)

1978

AIR CREW: #1 Maj Gord Wallis (Team Lead), #2 Capt Marc Ouellet, #3 Capt Wayne Thompson, #4 Capt Terry Hunt, #5 Capt Joe Molnar, #6 Capt Keith Coulter, #7 Capt John McNamara, #8 Capt Gord de Jong, #9 Capt Ray Hansford, #10 Capt Stuart Morgan, #11 Capt Yves Bosse, #12 Capt Jack Girard GROUND CREW: #1A Sgt Cec Keddy (Crew Chief), #2A MCpl Wally Corbin, #3A MCpl Garry Ward, #4A Cpl Ian Neilson, #5A Cpl Michel Poisson, #6A Cpl Al Dillman, #7A MCpl Kevin Buell, #8A MCpl Bob O'Reilly, #9A Cpl Fred Broderick, #10A Cpl John Zorn ADMIN: SG Richard (Civilian)

1979

AIR CREW: #1 Maj Tom Griffis (Team Lead), #2 Capt Marc Ouellet, #3 Capt Graham Miller, #4 Capt Terry Hunt, #5 Capt Jim Reith, #6 Capt Frank Thorne, #7 Capt John McNamara, #8 Capt Larry Rockliff, #9 Capt Ray Hansford, #10 Capt Yves Bosse, #11 Capt Jim Fowler, #12 Capt Ron Duckworth GROUND CREW: #1A Sgt Cec Keddy (Crew Chief), #2A MCpl Garry Ward, #3A MCpl Kevin Buell, #4A MCpl Ian Neilson, #5A Cpl Michel Bernier, #6A Cpl Fred Rockall, #7A Cpl Michel Roy, #8A Cpl Ed Gammon, #9A Cpl Michel Poisson, #10A Cpl Al Dillman ADMIN: SG Richard (Civilian)

1980

AIR CREW: #1 Maj Tom Griffis (Team Lead), #2 Capt Jim Gillespie, #3 Capt Graham Miller, #4 Capt Bob Drake, #5 Capt Yves Bosse, #6 Capt Frank Thorne, #7 Capt Wally Stone, #8 Capt Larry Rockliff, #9 Capt Dan Dempsey, #10 Capt Denis Mercier, #11 Capt Jim Fowler, #12 Capt Ron Duckworth GROUND CREW: #1A Sgt Don Simms (Crew Chief), #2A Cpl Al McGrath, #3A Cpl Rocky White, #4A Cpl Michel Langevin, #5A Cpl Jack Gariepy, #6A Cpl Ed Gammon, #7A Cpl Michel Bernier, #8A Cpl Michel Roy, #9A Cpl Fred Rockall, #10A MCpl Garry Ward, VOLUNTEER EXTRAS: Cpl Buell, MCpl Poisson, Cpl Bauer ADMIN: SG Richard (Civilian)/MJ Fowler (Civilian)

1981

AIR CREW: #1 Maj Mike Murphy (Team Lead) #2 Capt Jim Gillespie, #3 Capt Dennis Beselt, #4 Capt Bob Drake, #5 Capt Sonny Lefort, #6 Capt Dean Rainkie, #7 Capt Wally Stone, #8 Capt John Politis, #9 Capt Dan Dempsey, #10 Capt Denis Mercier, #11 Capt Wally Peters, #12 Capt Ron Duckworth/Lt Heather Campbell
GROUND CREW: #1A Sgt Don Simms (Crew Chief), #2A Cpl Paul McKeen, #3A MCpl George Beck, #4A Pte John McCanna, #5A Cpl Perry Luchia, #6A Cpl Tony Vanderberg, #7A Cpl Dick Bennett, #8A Cpl Bob Bauer, #9A Cpl Al McGrath, #10A Cpl Barry Fremont ADMIN: Marg Fowler (Civilian)

1982

AIR CREW: #1 Maj Mike Murphy (Team Lead), #2 Capt Geoff Gamble, #3 Capt Dennis Beselt, #4 Capt Tristan deKoninck, #5 Capt Sonny Lefort, #6 Capt Dean Rainkie, #7 Capt Rob Chapman, #8 Capt John Politis, #9 Capt Jon Graham, #10 Capt Ron Carter, #11 Maj Wally Peters, #12 Lt Heather Campbell/Capt Leslie Whan
GROUND CREW: #1A Sgt Alex Cameron (Crew Chief), #2A Cpl John McCanna, #3A Cpl Barry Fremont, #4A Cpl Dick Bennett, #5A Cpl Harry Partridge, #6A Cpl Bob Bauer, #7A Cpl Perry Luchia, #8A Cpl Marty Cornfield, #9A Cpl Tony Vanderberg, #11A MCpl George Beck, #12A Cpl Frank Pineau ADMIN: Marg Fowler (Civilian)

1983

AIR CREW: #1 Maj George Hawey (Team Lead), #2 Capt Geoff Gamble, #3 Capt Bill Ryan, #4 Capt Tristan deKoninck, #5 Capt Holmes Patton, #6 Capt Richie Clements, #7 Capt Rob Chapman, #8 Capt Bob Stephan, #9 Capt Jon Graham, #10 Capt Ron Carter, #11 Maj Norm Fraser, #12 Capt Leslie Whan GROUND CREW: #1A Sgt Alex Cameron (Crew Chief), #2A Cpl Mike Landers, #3A MCpl Bill MacPhee, #4A Cpl Pat Messaoud, #5A Cpl Georges Menard, #6A Cpl Harry Partridge, #7A Pte Tim Payne, #8A Cpl Marty Cornfield, #9A Cpl Ron Bernard, #10A Cpl Bob Bauer, #12A Cpl Frank Pineau ADMIN: Marg Fowler (Civilian)

AIR CREW: #1 Maj George Hawey (Team Lead), #2 Capt Al Merrick, #3 Capt Bill Ryan, #4 Capt Dave Forman, #5 Capt Holmes Patton, #6 Capt Richie Clements, #7 Capt Carl Shaver, #8 Capt Bob Stephan, #9 Capt Steve Wallace, #10 Capt Mike Bell, #11 Maj Norm Fraser, #12 Capt Leslie Whan GROUND CREW: #1A Sgt Rick Harvey (Crew Chief), #2A MCpl Mike Landers, #3A MCpl Bill MacPhee, #4A Cpl Pat Messaoud, #5A Cpl Georges Menard, #6A Cpl Doug Dennison, #7A Cpl Rene Petit, #8A Cpl Dan Jean- Marie, #9A Cpl Ron Bernard, #11A Cpl Tim Payne, #12A Cpl Frank Pineau ADMIN: Marg Fowler (Civilian)

AIR CREW: #1 Maj Yogi Huyghebaert (Team Lead), #2 Capt Al Merrick, #3 Capt Steve Purton, #4 Capt Dave Forman, #5 Capt Gino Tessier, #6 Capt Steve Hill, #7 Capt Carl Shaver, #8 Capt Mike Skubicky, #9 Capt Steve Wallace, #10 Capt Mike Bell, #11 Capt Eric Dumont, #12 Capt Leslie Whan GROUND CREW: #1A Sgt Rick Harvey (Crew Chief), #2A Cpl Mark Keller, #3A MCpl Brian Herde, #4A Cpl Bert Hargreaves, #5A Cpl Al Herron, #6A Cpl Doug Dennison, #7A Cpl Rene St- Laurent, #8A Cpl Dan Jean- Marie, #9A Cpl John Mahoney, #10A Cpl Rene Petit, #12A Cpl Troy Canam ADMIN: Marg Fowler (Civilian)

AIR CREW: #1 Maj Yogi Huyghebaert (Team Lead), #2 Capt Joe Parente, #3 Capt Steve Purton, #4 Capt Jim Fowlow, #5 Capt Gino Tessier, #6 Capt Steve Hill, #7 Capt Howard Tarbet, #8 Capt Mike Skubicky, #9 Capt Don Brodeur, #10 Capt Bob Curran/Capt Richard LaPointe, #11 Capt Eric Dumont, #12 Capt Leslie Whan/Capt Ross Fetterly GROUND CREW: #1A Sgt Alex Bouzane (Crew Chief), #2A Cpl Mark Keller, #3A MCpl Brian Herde, #4A Cpl Don Brak/ Cpl Bill Dennis, #5A Cpl Al Herron, #6A Cpl Mark Doane, #7A Cpl Gilles Dube, #8A Cpl Gord Neave, #9A Cpl John Mahoney, #11A Cpl Bert Hargreaves, #12A Cpl Troy Canam ADMIN: Marg Fowler (Civilian)

1987

AIR CREW: #1 Maj Dave Wilson/Maj Dennis Beselt (Team Lead), #2 Capt Joe Parente, #3 Capt Paul Giles, #4 Capt Jim Fowlow, #5 Capt Don Barnby, #6 Capt Boyd Smith, #7 Capt Howard Tarbet, #8 Capt Wes MacKay, #9 Capt Don Brodeur, #10 Capt Richard Lapointe, #11 Capt Eric Dumont, #12 Capt Ross Fetterly
GROUND CREW: #1A WO Alex Bouzane (Crew Chief), #2A MCpl Dan Bergeron, #3A Cpl Mike Cook, #4A Cpl Chris Detta, #5A Cpl Wally Marshall, #6A Cpl Mark Doane, #7A Cpl Gilles Dube, #8A Cpl Gord Neave, #9A Cpl Serge Pilote, #11A Cpl Brian Duivenvoorde, #12A Cpl Darren Schuszter ADMIN: Marg Fowler (Civilian)

1988

AIR CREW: #1 Maj Dennis Beselt (Team Lead), #2 Capt Shane Antaya, #3 Capt Paul Giles, #4 Capt Bjorn Kjaer, #5 Capt Don Barnby, #6 Capt Boyd Smith, #7 Capt Darryl Shyiak, #8 Capt Wes MacKay, #9 Capt Ken Rae, #10 Capt Richard Lapointe, #11 Capt Kevin Kokotailo, #12 Capt Ross Fetterly GROUND CREW: #1A Sgt Jerry Unrau (Crew Chief), #2A Cpl Mike Cook, #3A MCpl Guy Fortin, #4A Cpl Serge Pilote, #5A Cpl Marc Cossette, #6A MCpl Oswald Lindsay, #7A Cpl Walter Marshall, #8A Cpl Denis Fontaine, #9A MCpl Dan Bergeron, #10A Cpl Chris Detta, #12A Cpl Darren Schuszter ADMIN: Marg Fowler (Civilian)

1989

AIR CREW: #1 Maj Dan Dempsey (Team Lead), #2 Capt Shane Antaya, #3 Capt Stephen Will, #4 Capt Bjorn Kjaer, #5 Capt John Low, #6 Capt Dale Hackett, #7 Capt Darryl Shyiak, #8 Capt Les Racicot, #9 Capt Bob Stephan, #10 Capt Dominic Taillon, #11 Capt Kevin Kokotailo, #12 Capt Ross Fetterly GROUND CREW: #1A Sgt Jerry Unrau (Crew Chief), #2A MCpl Mario Deshaies, #3A MCpl Guy Fortin, #4A Cpl Jim Burton, #5A Cpl Marc Cossette, #6A MCpl Oswald Lindsay, #7A Cpl Dave Scharf, #8A MCpl Doug Dennison, #9A Cpl Leo Jenkins, #11A Cpl Denis Fontaine, #12A L/S Darcy Gallipeau ADMIN: Marg Fowler (Civilian)

1990

AIR CREW: #1 Maj Dan·Dempsey (Team Lead), #2 Capt Ross Granley, #3 Capt Stephen Will, #4 Capt Vince Jandrisch, #5 Capt John Low, #6 Capt Dale Hackett, #7 Capt Brooke Lawrence, #8 Capt Les Racicot, #9 Capt Rich Lancaster, #10 Capt Dominic Taillon, #11 Capt Jeff Hill, #12 Capt Ross Fetterly/Capt Paul Richards
GROUND CREW: #1A Sgt Dan Bergeron (Crew Chief), #2A MCpl Mario Deshaies, #3A Cpl Tony Edmundson, #4A Cpl Jim Burton, #5A Cpl Dan Seguin, #6A Cpl Rick Macnab, #7A Cpl Dave Scharf, #8A Sgt Doug Dennison, #9A Cpl Leo Jenkins, #10A MCpl Dave Fischer, #12A L/S Darcy Gallipeau ADMIN: Marg Fowler (Civilian)

BILL JOHNSON

1991

AIR CREW: #1 Maj Bob Stephan (Team·Lead), #2 Capt Ross Granley, #3 Capt Marc Robert, #4. Capt Vince Jandrisch, #5 Capt Nick Cassidy, #6 Capt Bill Watts, #7 Capt Brooke Lawrence, #8 Capt Glenn Oerzen, #9 Capt Rich Lancaster, #10 Capt Real Turgeon, #11 Capt Jeff Hill, #12 Capt Paul Richards GROUND CREW: #1A Sgt Dan Bergeron (Crew Chief), #2A Cpl Marco Asselin, #3A Cpl Tony Edmundson, #4A Cpl Rick Murray, #5A Cpl Dan Seguin, #6A Cpl Rick Macnab, #7A Cpl Doug Wray, #8A MCpl Dave Fischer, #9A MCpl Ed Dillon, #11A Cpl Stewart Gilchrist, #12A L/S Darcy Gallipeau ADMIN: Marg Fowler (Civilian)

1992

AIR CREW: #1 Maj Bob Stephan (Team Lead), #2 Capt Rob Martin, #3 Capt Marc Robert, #4 Capt Glen Kerr, #5 Capt Nick Cassidy, #6 Capt Bill Watts, #7 Capt Frank Bergnach, #8 Capt Glenn Oerzen, #9 Capt Bob Painchaud, #10 Capt Real Turgeon, #11 Capt Mike Lenehan, #12 Capt Paul Richards GROUND CREW: #1A Sgt Joe Maillet (Crew Chief), #2A MCpl Stewart Gilchrist/Cpl Mike Crickmore, #3A Cpl Mike Ubell, #4A Cpl Rick Murray, #5A Cpl Vince Leather, #6A Cpl Terry Spence, #7A Cpl Doug Wray, #8A Cpl Marco Asselin, #9A MCpl Ed Dillon, #10A Cpl Kori Ibey, #12A Cpl Earle Bourgeois ADMIN: Marg Fowler (Civilian)

The Snowbirds

They swoop, and dive, then climb once more,
as if to knock at Heaven's door.
Alas, they pass us, on the run,
They're our high flight -- they're our Top Guns.

When the 431 A.D.S. flies,
they're our ambassadors of the skies.
They've shown to us, and to the rest,
there is no doubt, they are the best!

twenty-five years

AIR CREW: #1 Maj Dean Rainkie (Team Lead), #2 Capt Rob Martin, #3 Capt Andre Lortie, #4 Capt Glen Kerr, #5 Capt Dean Mosher, #6 Capt Chris Granley, #7 Capt Frank Bergnach, #8 Capt Michel Cliche, #9 Capt Bob Painchaud, #10 Capt Francois Cousineau/Capt Menes Pierre- Pierre, #11 Capt Mike Lenehan, #12 Capt Paul Richards/Capt Tana Beer GROUND CREW: #1A Sgt Joe Maillet (Crew Chief), #2A Cpl Pierre Turgeon, #3A Cpl Mike Ubell, #4A Cpl Denis Houde, #5A Cpl Vince Leather, #6A Cpl Terry Spence, #7A Cpl Marlene Shillingford, #8A Cpl Kori Ibey, #9A MCpl Jim Flach, #11A Cpl Mike Crickmore, #12A Cpl Earle Bourgeois ADMIN: Marg Fowler (Civilian)

RICK RADELL

AIR CREW: #1 Maj Dean Rainkie (Team Lead), #2 Capt Mario Hamel, #3 Capt Andre Lortie, #4 Capt Will McEwan, #5 Capt Derek Mosher, #6 Capt Chris Granley, #7 Capt Dave Deere, #8 Capt Michel Cliche, #9 Capt Norm Dequier, #10 Capt Menes Pierre- Pierre, #11 Capt Mike Lenehan, #12 Capt Tana Beer GROUND CREW: #1A Sgt Mark Doane (Crew Chief), #2A Cpl Pierre Turgeon, #3A Cpl Rick Ouellette, #4A Cpl Denis Houde, #5A Cpl Richard Jack, #6A Cpl Mike Crickmore, #7A Cpl Marlene Shillingford, #8A Cpl Gord Tulloch, #9A MCpl Jim Flach, #11A Cpl Ron Kleim, #12A Cpl Earle Bourgeois/Cpl Liz Vella ADMIN: Marg Fowler (Civilian)

AIR CREW: #1 Maj Steve Hill (Team Lead), #2 Capt Mario Hamel, #3 Capt Greg Carlow, #4 Capt Will McEwan, #5 Capt Jeff Young, #6 Capt Ian Searle, #7 Capt Dave Deere, #8 Capt Steve Dion, #9 Capt Norm Dequier, #10 Capt Menes Pierre- Pierre, #11 Capt Claude Lebel, #12 Capt Tana Beer GROUND CREW: #1A Sgt Mark Doane (Crew Chief), #2A Cpl Tony Solimine, #3A Cpl Tim Woodward, #4A Cpl Dan De Luca, #5A Cpl Richard Jack, #6A Cpl Rick Ouellette, #7A Cpl Ron Kleim, #8A Cpl Gord Tulloch, #9A MCpl Martin Singher, #10A Cpl Eric Bissonnette, #11A Cpl Liz Vella ADMIN: Marg Fowler (Civilian)